Michael Leunig was born in East Melbourne in 1945. He began drawing cartoons for newspapers in 1965. His work appears regularly in the Melbourne *Age* and the *Sydney Morning Herald*. He is married and has four children.

His other books include *The Penguin Leunig*, *The Second Leunig*, *A Bag of Roosters*, *Ramming the Shears*, *The Travelling Leunig*, *A Common Prayer*, *The Prayer Tree*, *The Michael Leunig Collection*, *Everyday Devils and Angels*, *A Bunch of Poesy*, *You and Me*, *Why Dogs Sniff Each Other's Tails* and *Goatperson*.

Short
Notes

from the Long History of happiness

Michael Leunig

Viking

Published by the Penguin Group
Penguin Books Australia Ltd, 250 Camberwell Road, Camberwell, Victoria, 3124, Australia
Penguin Books Ltd, 80 Strand, London WC2R 0RL, England
Penguin Putnam Inc., 375 Hudson Street, New York, New York 10014, USA
Penguin Books, a division of Pearson Canada, 10 Alcorn Avenue, Toronto, Ontario, Canada M4V 3B2
Penguin Books (NZ) Ltd, Cnr Rosedale and Airborne Roads, Albany, Auckland, New Zealand
Penguin Books (South Africa) (Pty) Ltd, 24 Sturdee Avenue, Rosebank, Johannesburg 2196, South Africa
Penguin Books India (P) Ltd, 11, Community Centre, Panchsheel Park, New Delhi 110 017, India

First published by Penguin Books Australia Ltd 1996
15 14 13 12 11 10 9 8
Copyright © Michael Leunig 1996. Illustrations copyright © Michael Leunig 1996

Typeset in 10/14 Gill Sans Light by Midland Typesetters. Printed and bound by South China Co. Ltd, Hong Kong/China

National Library of Australia Cataloguing-in-Publication data:
Leunig, Michael, 1945– .
Short notes from the long history of happiness.

ISBN 0 670 87405 1.

1. Caricatures and cartoons – Australia. 2. Australian wit and humor. Pictorial. I. Title.

741.5994

Acknowledgements

I would like to thank George Dale for all his help.

The publishers would like to thank HarperCollins Publishers for permission to reprint material from *The Second Leunig: A Dusty Little Swag, A Bunch of Poesy* and *A Bag of Roosters.*

The prayers 'God give us rain when we expect sun', 'There are only two feelings. Love and fear', 'We struggle, we grow weary, we grow tired', 'We celebrate spring's returning and the rejuvenation of the natural world', 'The path to your door' and 'Love one another and you will be happy' are taken from *A Common Prayer* published by HarperCollins*Religious*, Melbourne, 1990.

The prayers 'Love is born', 'God help us to live slowly', 'In order to be truthful', 'We rejoice and give thanks for earthworms', 'We give thanks for the blessing of winter', 'God bless those who suffer from the common cold' and 'We give thanks for our friends' are taken from *The Prayer Tree* published by HarperCollins*Religious*, Melbourne, 1991.

Reproduction of 'Birds passing on the secrets of the universe to sleeping baby' with permission of National Gallery of Victoria, Melbourne.

www.penguin.com.au

The long history of happiness is unrecorded
And shall remain so forever,
Yet it can be known completely.

A few short notes, however, have been made:

Happiness is the child of Love and Truth,
Who struggled just to live yet found each other;
And in the crib of all their weariness
Their little happiness lay sleeping.

Michael Leunig

Courting couple

Spring Love Poem.

When first we met my love and I
Took shelter from the rainy sky
Beneath a crispy, gold baguette
Which bended as it did get wet.

It bended gently and it drooped
Upon our love as there we stooped
And sheltered from the storm above:
A soggy, golden crown of love.

The sun came out; the piece of bread
Lay at our feet all limp and dead.
Greater love. Lest we forget.
My love and I. The wet baguette.

Leunig

Spring Diary of a Small, Brown Bird.

It is a perfect, sunny day.
I am standing on the grass
singing when suddenly, out of
the blue, he arrives

He lands beside me, throws
out his chest and launches into
such a beautiful song; so loud
and clear. What a voice!
WHAT A VOICE!

I turn away to conceal my
rush of delight and he
proceeds to prance boldly in a circle
around me with one extended
wing beating softly and
rhythmically at the earth.

Such skill and balance! What zest! What a thrilling dance! I cannot help myself. I push my breast against the ground and raise my tail to the splendour of the sun. He appears to love me.

Closer and closer he circles. I yearn. I spin. I swoon. Tenderly he closes in on me sideways. His eyes sparkle like pitch. Our beaks meet. Our feathers merge. I am in paradise.

What happens next I can't remember Bliss is the sweetest form of unconsciousness.

Now, all I want to do is to love him and to gather small twigs and carry them to some high and peaceful place where I can build and listen to my heart.

Leunig

OLD RECIPE, NEW RECIPE: THE KITCHEN OF GIVE AND TAKE.

FIRST YOU MUST CLIMB INTO THE BATTERED OLD SAUCEPAN OF LOVE WHERE YOU WILL MARINATE IN THE SAUCE OF SEX.

THEN YOU SHALL BE COVERED WITH THE WINE OF FAITH, THE OIL OF COMPASSION AND THE SALT OF SIN AND SUFFERING.

NOW YOU ARE TOSSED IN THE PAN OF CHAOS AND SEARED BY THE FLAME OF TRUTH

YOU ARE CARVED BY THE
KNIFE OF COMPROMISE AND
SERVED WITH THE SPOON
OF DUTY;

ONTO THE PLATE OF
ACCEPTANCE AND GARNISHED
WITH THE HERBS OF HUMILITY.

AT THIS POINT YOU
MAY WELL SAY GRACE.

leunig

In Order to Be Truthful

In order to be truthful
We must do more than speak the truth.
We must also hear truth.
We must also receive truth.
We must also act upon truth.
We must also search for truth.
The difficult truth.
Within us and around us.
We must devote ourselves to truth.
Otherwise we are dishonest
And our lives are mistaken.
God grant us the strength and the courage
To be truthful.
Amen

BASIC PRINCIPLES OF GOAT HUSBANDRY.

Was it on your wedding day that you first thought your husband was a goat?

— that you had married into a family of goats?

or was it on your wedding night when you found him on top of the wardrobe butting his horns at the light bulb?

Or was it the arrival of the first child that confirmed your suspicions?

Or was it when your clothing began to disappear?

Goats are difficult, certainly, but cheer up, — goats are good and honest too; they mean well; they are funny, courageous and loving. Better to be married to a goat than a fox!

Have you seen my pyjamas anywhere?

oh dear, I'm sorry; I think I <u>ate</u> them.

Leunig

God help us to live slowly:
To move simply:
To look softly:
To allow emptiness:
To let the heart create for us.
Amen

FAVORITE WORN AND SHABBY DOMESTIC ITEMS

THE ARMCHAIR OF PHILOSOPHY.   THE TEAPOT OF TRUTH.   THE PILLOW OF FAITH.

THE RUG OF CONSTANCY.

THE VASE OF TRANQUILLITY

THE DOG OF SANITY

Leunig

MY BIG TOE

My big toe is an honest man
So down to earth and normal;
Always true unto himself
And pleasantly informal;
Full of simple energy.
Contented with his role.
If all of me was more like him
I'd be a happy soul.

Leunig

Leunig

A HERBAL Remedy for LIFEACHE.

you suffer
from lifeache

your whole life
is sore; it hurts
when you move it.

HERBAL REMEDY.
Take one patch of
grass, a mild day
and two large, green trees.

Lie on the grass beneath one tree and contemplate the other tree.

nap from time to time or gaze occasionally at the grass.

Pain will subside. Lifeache <u>cannot</u> be cured but you can learn to <u>MANAGE THE SYMPTOMS</u>.

Leunig

Prayer for Friends

We give thanks for our friends.
Our dear friends.
We anger each other.
We fail each other.
We share this sad earth, this tender life, this precious time.
Such richness. Such wildness.
Together we are blown about.
Together we are dragged along.
All this delight.
All this suffering.
All this forgiving life.
We hold it together.
Amen

HOW YOU WILL KNOW IF A PERSON

(PERHAPS A POLITICIAN, A POLICEMAN, A PARTNER OR A PRIEST) IS CORRUPT.

you must study the duck.
you must play with the duck.
you must talk with the duck.
you must know the ways of the duck.

You must look deeply
into the eyes of the duck

Then looking into the face of
the person, how will you know
if that person is corrupt?

You will know.
YOU WILL KNOW.

Leunig

NEAR-DEATH EXPERIENCE

He had heard of near-death experiences and their transforming power but he had never had one.

It seemed to him that much of humanity was near death; the way people watched so much television!
"The living dead" he thought.

While out walking it occurred to him that modern existence itself might be a constant, near-death experience.

A flower truck turned a corner and a load of daffodils spilled from the back and buried him.

He lay bewildered for a moment under the glowing yellow heap and then poked his head out into the sunshine.

He saw his reflection in a shop window. He smelled the daffodils.
"How lovely!" he thought.
It was a <u>near-life</u> experience and already a transformation was in progress.

Leunig

Prayer of Gratitude

We rejoice and give thanks for earthworms, bees, ladybirds and broody hens; for humans tending their gardens, talking to animals, cleaning their homes and singing to themselves; for the rising of the sap, the fragrance of growth, the invention of the wheelbarrow and the existence of the teapot we give thanks. We celebrate and give thanks.
Amen

AROMATHERAPIES - TRIED AND TRUE

Essence of fish and
chips

essence of shoe
polish

essence of
wheat bag

essence of wet
dog

essence of burnt
toast

essence of saturday
afternoon

essence of clean
sheets.

essence of sweetheart

leunig

ATMOSPHERE

HOW TO BE OF VALUE

Stare into a bucket of
water until your
reflection appears.

Then gently pour the
reflection out onto the
ground.

Soon it will evaporate

and become a cloud.

Then it will rain

and you will be part of the great cycle of refreshment and growth.

A man meets twelve great spiritual leaders

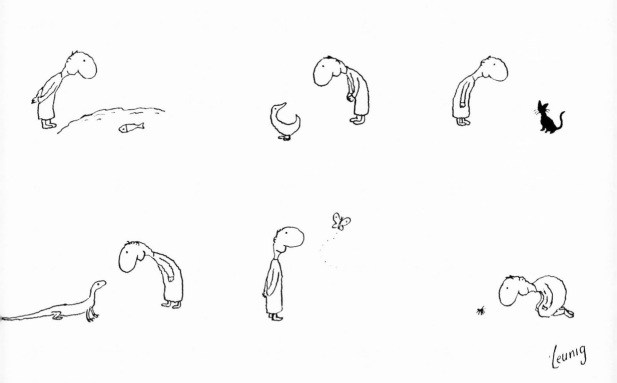

leunig

SOMETHING OF VALUE

One sunny day you look down and there it is at your feet... a tiny piece of gold.

You pick it up and as you do you notice the vein in a rock where it came from

Excitedly you begin to dig .... you follow the vein downwards.

Down, down.... away from the sun... you work earnestly and the years pass.

Deeper you follow
the lead. Smashing
at the rock face....
propping the tunnel...
exhausting yourself.

You begin to fear
a cave-in and by now
it is too dark to see
the gold.

All you can do is
feel its weight in
your hands.

Back on the surface
is another beautiful
sunny day..... the
same as it ever was.

Leunig

'Love one another and you will be happy.'
It's as simple and as difficult as that. There is
no other way.
Amen

HOW TO SLEEP WELL ☽

"GOOD PYJAMAS : GOOD SLEEP",
so goes the old saying, yet many
people do not understand the
vital significance of pyjamas in
the achievement of deep and
restful sleep

SLEEPING IS A RELIGIOUS ACTIVITY: a holy
communion with the inner world of dreams
and darkness. The appropriate ceremonial
attire is important for a smooth
passage into the land of nod

ESSENTIALLY, PYJAMAS MUST FEEL
COMFORTABLE AND LOOK RIDICULOUS.
Wearing them is a ritualistic
renunciation of the conscious,
external world: the world of
looking good and feeling stressed.

As we approach the cot, pyjama clad, the LUDICROUS SELF is proclaimed, triumphant and free. The vestments of the outer world lie cast off and crumpled on the floor.

We look soft and child-like; inept and shambling; primitive and funny. The pyjama fabric droops like tired old elephant skin. The buttons are done up in the wrong holes. The trousers are hitched up nearly to the arm pits. The cuffs wag above the ankles.

One side of the coat is tucked in; the other side hangs out. We have no place in the "real" world looking like this! WE ARE THE STUFF THAT DREAMS ARE MADE OF. What freedom! What peace! What blessed relief! "GOOD PYJAMAS: GOOD SLEEP."

Leunig

A LITTLE MAN IS A WONDERFUL COMPANION AND CAN BE PURCHASED FROM ANY REPUTABLE PET SHOP.

WHEN CHOOSING A LITTLE MAN FROM A BATCH, SELECT THE MOST BOISTEROUS: THE ONE WHO PUSHES THE OTHERS ASIDE AS HE RUSHES TO GREET YOU

LIFT HIM FROM THE PEN AND PLACE HIM ON THE SHOP FLOOR FOR OBSERVATION. LOOK FOR THE FOLLOWING: A NICE BRIGHT PRANCE, PLAYFUL AGGRESSION AND RESPONSIVENESS TO AFFECTION.

UPON GETTING YOUR LITTLE MAN HOME
ALLOW HIM TO EXPLORE HIS NEW
TERRITORY AND GIVE HIM A NAME,
PREFERABLY WITH TWO SYLLABLES.

IF HE CRIES IN THE NIGHT GIVE
HIM A HOT WATER BOTTLE. DON'T
CHASTISE HIM UNDULY, AFTER ALL,
HE'S JUST A LITTLE MAN.

TAKE HIM FOR A WALK, TALK
TO HIM, LOOK AFTER HIM; HE'LL
REWARD YOU WITH MANY HAPPY
YEARS OF LOYAL COMPANIONSHIP.

Leunig

YOU KNOW
WHAT I
HATE ABOUT
YOU...?

IT'S YOUR
UGLY ELEPHANT
TRUNK I HATE...!

Leunig

The child in Spring

Leunig

<u>The lost art of <u>WINE QUAFFING</u></u>

A good wine quaffer is rarely seen these days. QUAFFING, true quaffing, requires SKILL and DARING.

Special QUAFFING WINE is required to produce the essential and distinctive "QUAFF!" sound as the wine passes from the mouth down into the gullet.

The genuine quaffing sound can best be described as a sound composed of the following elements—AIR, LIQUID, BULK and HOLLOWNESS. A mysterious combination of these four sound qualities is the rich, alluring hypnotic sound of <u>QUAFFING</u> and once heard can never be forgotten.

CROSS SECTION
↓

The wine is taken boldly through slightly parted lips into a mouth poised in a cavernous manner (which produces the necessary sound chamber) The rushing wine slaps against the back of the mouth and folds over into a small wave. It is important that the tongue lie flat and motionless on the floor of the mouth so as not to impede the natural draining action. The gullet is suddenly opened just as the small wave flops and breaks on the "rapids" created by the TONSILS.

AIR RUSHES INTO THE MOUTH TO FILL THE GAP WHERE THE WINE WAS. THIS "WHOOSHING" COMBINES WITH THE ECHO OF THE BREAKING WAVE AND THE GARGLING-FLUSHING SOUND. A WELL ROUNDED, CLEARLY DISTINGUISHABLE "QUAFF" IS THUS PRODUCED.

Leunig

God give us rain when we expect sun.
Give us music when we expect trouble.
Give us tears when we expect breakfast.
Give us dreams when we expect a storm.
Give us a stray dog when we expect congratulations.
God play with us, turn us sideways and around.
Amen

HOW TO GET THERE

Go to the end of the path until you get to the gate.

Go through the gate and head straight out towards the horizon.

Keep going towards the horizon.

Sit down and have
a rest every now
and again.

But keep on going.
Just keep on with it.

Keep on going as
far as you can.
That's how you
get there

Leunig

THE OLD, OLD DOG.

"Buy me!"
"Buy me!" yelled the
products, but he couldn't
hear them any more.

"Watch me!" cried
the television.
"Read me!" cried the
magazines but he couldn't
hear them any more.

"Drive me!" screamed
the car.
"Notice me" shrieked
the celebrity but he
couldn't hear them
any more.

"Hello" said a gentle voice, and hearing it he turned to see an old dog.

"Hello and welcome to a new part of your life", said the old dog smiling at him.

"It won't be very flash", said the old dog "and it wouldn't rate very highly on an opinion poll but there'll be loyalty and warmth and time enough to rest" said the old, old dog.

The Common Cold

God bless those who suffer from the common cold.
Nature has entered into them;
Has led them aside and gently lain them low
To contemplate life from the wayside;
To consider human frailty;
To receive the deep and dreamy messages of fever.
We give thanks for the insights of this humble perspective.
We give thanks for blessings in disguise.
Amen

Is Gambolling a Vice........ or a Folly?

Gambolling is **NOT** a **VICE**. **GAMBOLLING** is Very **NICE**.

FRISKING, FROLLICKING and gleeful DANCING

Nor is gambolling a **FOLLY**. Gambolling is good and **JOLLY**.

Skipping, Rollicking and Felicitous RAMBLING:

ROMPING, CAPERING and PRANCING

SUCH is the nature of good old GAMBOLLING.

Leunig

THE CAT CAME BACK

The whole thing began because of overpopulation, war and a global ecological disaster...

which led to a complete breakdown of law and order and an outbreak of violent crime on a massive scale.

which led to universal demoralisation and a catastrophic worldwide economic depression

which meant that he lost his job and began squabbling with his wife

which caused him, one morning, to go out and kick the dog which bit the cat and ate its food.

causing the cat to leave home in a huff and hide under the neighbour's house for three days

THREE DAYS !! for three days they fretted and pined and nobody slept a wink until....

The cat came back. Blessed relief ! The cat returned home.

Leunig

ON THE MEND.

Things were getting too fast; too careless; too dangerous. People were breaking up and breaking down. The footpath was dividing and crumbling. He was afraid.

He lost his nerve. He tripped and stumbled. He cried out and fell back; backwards into his own mouth; down into his deep cry for help.

Down and down he fell, swallowed up by his own darkness. Deeper and deeper, darker and darker until he lost consciousness

And there he dreamed of
a woman who embraced him
completely ; who bathed him
peacefully ; who blessed him
simply .

He awoke and arose in
the sunlight from out of
the back of his trousers.
Totally refreshed; utterly
secure ; perfectly serene.

It was definitely a strange
situation and there was still
much work to be done but
he felt sure that life
was on the mend.

Leunig

Dear God,
We celebrate spring's returning and the rejuvenation of the natural world. Let us be moved by this vast and gentle insistence that goodness shall return, that warmth and life shall succeed, and help us to understand our place within this miracle. Let us see that as a bird now builds its nest, bravely, with bits and pieces, so we must build human faith. It is our simple duty; it is the highest art; it is our natural and vital role within the miracle of spring: the creation of faith.
Amen

He was a sailor
but the sea was not
around him; it was
inside him!

A vast deep ocean
inside him and on it
his heart was adrift
and alone.

Powerful currents
pulled him this way
and that; pulled him
off course

Wild storms when
sick and afraid he
held on for dear life

Calm days when he
drifted in peace. Still
nights when he steered
by the stars and heard
angels singing across
the water.

How long he had sailed.
How little he understood
the sea. In the dark
depths, unknown to him,
mysterious, black shapes
glided and prowled. He
was a sailor and the
sea was inside him!

Leunig

Humanity is in
decline. Day by
day we become
more horrible
and foolish.

I want to confess
to you that I feel
ashamed of my species.
We are truly appalling.
I am deeply,
bitterly sorry
and sad.

Our failure is
unforgivable
I am sick with guilt:
exhausted and
empty from
worrying about
it.

I beg you: please
condemn me with a
look, growl at me,
discontinue your loyalty.
I offer you my hands.
<u>PLEASE BITE THEM</u>..

Leunig

In my life I had
accumulated many things
in my head...
TOO MANY THINGS...!

Memories, tunes, facts,
fears, visions, loves...
etc etc...as many
as possible

In a fertile mind such
things will interbreed.
mongrel visions are born
... hybrid memories...
inbred, idiot love....
It gets very **CONFUSING**

I decided it was
time for a good
cleanup so I emptied
it all out of my head
and pushed it up in
a big heap to sort
it out.

There it was... everything that was me, all in a big jumbled heap. I walked around it. What a mess...!

Then suddenly I saw it in silhouette and realized what it was.... IT WAS A HEAP.... A SIMPLE HEAP...! you don't sort it out... you climb it... you climb it because it is there...

Excitedly I clambered to the summit and raised a flag. I was now looking beyond everything that I knew.

THE VIEW WAS SIMPLY MAGNIFICENT

COMMON SENSE

Cross my heart, I remember
when common sense was
delivered to the door each
morning by horse and cart —

Equally to the rich and poor. What
a bold start it was to find
it sitting there on the porch—
all yours, fresh as a daisy
and as good as gold.

Completely undebated, was
common sense — unprocessed
you might say: full of organisms
and rough seeds; it's what the
body needs.... you could feel
it do you good.

How could such a useful thing—
so plentiful back then yet so
revered — become so lost
and rare; and SO <u>WEIRD</u>?

you have to go through so
much these days — crawl
across a field of broken bottles
— half a life of suffering and
sin — be done over and
done in.....

...Before you find it once again.
Perhaps one morning — on the
porch and in the sun of early
spring — lo and behold — on
the step — thank Christ! —
a little common sense is
there again.

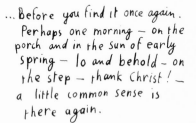

Leunig

The Path to Your Door

The path to your door
Is the path within:
Is made by animals,
Is lined by flowers,
Is lined by thorns,
Is stained with wine,
Is lit by the lamp of sorrowful dreams:
Is washed with joy,
Is swept by grief,
Is blessed by the lonely traffic of art:
Is known by heart,
Is known by prayer,
Is lost and found,
Is always strange,
The path to your door.

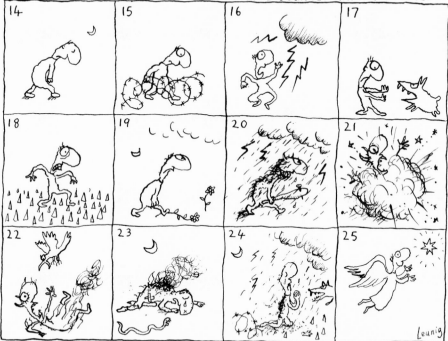

How to prepare the turkey.

Approach the turkey calmly
and STEADILY. Speak gently
and frankly about your
intentions.

Sit quietly and listen to
the turkey. You might hear
something you hadn't considered.
Be prepared to alter your plans.

Don't push the discussion
too hard. Take a break and
arrange a further meeting —
perhaps in a small café;
somewhere cheery and relaxed.

Stroll together; along a beach, through a park, down a cobbled lane. Continue to talk and listen — a strolling conversation is more real; it has a special dignity; it has a poetic outcome.

Sit side by side and watch the sun set. Watch the stars come out. Travel together and tell each other of your dreams. Open up your hearts and take comfort in being together.

You will not have Christmas dinner, but so what,— you will have peace, divine fellowship and most importantly, a feathered friend.

Leunig

SHOULD CHILDREN BELIEVE IN SANTA....?   SHOULD SANTA BELIEVE IN CHILDREN...?

DOES CHILDHOOD REALLY EXIST
OR IS IT JUST AN OLD CHRISTMAS
LEGEND...?

AND IF IT EXISTS; IS IT
INHABITED BY ACTUAL <u>CHILDREN</u>.?
INNOCENT, HOPEFUL CHILDREN.?

TRUSTING BELIEVERS.....
SAVIOURS AND RENEWERS...
THE GREATEST LOVERS...
THE SWEETEST DREAMERS..?

ONE PERSON, SANTA CLAUS,
STILL BELIEVES IN ALL THESE
THINGS AND EACH CHRISTMAS NIGHT
HE GOES OUT SEARCHING FOR AS
MANY SUCH CHILDREN AS HE CAN FIND

HE TIP-TOES INTO THEIR HOMES
JUST FOR THE LOVE OF SEEING
THEM SLEEPING.
HE IS SO GRATEFUL FOR
THEIR EXISTENCE THAT HE
LEAVES GIFTS

OCCASIONALLY EVEN SANTA
HAS HIS DOUBTS. TO HIM
IT SOMETIMES ALL SEEMS
TOO GOOD TO BE TRUE.

Christmas

I see a twinkle in your eye.
So this shall be my Christmas star
And I will travel to your heart:
The manger where the real things are.

And I will find a mother there
Who holds you gently to her breast;
A father to protect your peace;
And by these things you shall be blessed.

And you will always be reborn;
And I will always see the star
And make the journey to your heart:
The manger where the real things are.

THE BOTTLE

I met a man perched on a bottle
With a woman deep inside;
Rising slowly up towards him,
Floating on the tears he cried.

Said he, "It's only tears can save her;
Tears of sorrow: tears of pain.
I'm going to have to feel a lot
Until I have her back again"

All sniffling and snuffling
He said "It almost makes me laugh;
To think that if you weep enough
A man can find his better half."

Leunig

Love

Love is born
With a dark and troubled face
When hope is dead
And in the most unlikely place
Love is born:
Love is always born.

Winter

We give thanks for the blessing of winter:
Season to cherish the heart.
To make warmth and quiet for the heart.
To make soups and broths for the heart.
To cook for the heart and read for the heart.
To curl up softly and nestle with the heart.
To sleep deeply and gently at one with the heart.
To dream with the heart.
To spend time with the heart.
A long, long time of peace with the heart.
We give thanks for the blessing of winter:
Season to cherish the heart.
Amen

Birds passing on the secrets of the universe to sleeping baby

Leunig

We struggle, we grow weary, we grow tired.
We are exhausted, we are distressed, we
despair. We give up, we fall down, we let go.
We cry. We are empty, we grow calm, we are
ready. We wait quietly.

A small, shy truth arrives. Arrives from
without and within. Arrives and is born.
Simple, steady, clear. Like a mirror, like a
bell, like a flame. Like rain in summer. A
precious truth arrives and is born within us.
Within our emptiness.

We accept it, we observe it, we absorb it.
We surrender to our bare truth. We are
nourished, we are changed. We are blessed.
We rise up.

For this we give thanks.
Amen

Let it go. Let it out.
Let it all unravel.
Let it free and it can be
A path on which to travel.

The Grand Picnic

A SPECIAL POEM FOR ME BUT IT CAN BE FOR YOU ALSO IF YOU LIKE.

Each day — such a fuss.
Such praise, such damnation.

Ooh, ahh, yes, no.
Exhaustion and disintegration.

Such a fuss, yet the goat
Eats little flowers and thorns

And hears the sparrow....
Singing brightly in his horns,

(The sun is sweet; the
afternoon lies sleeping
in the valley.)

A song "for little flowers and thorns
Digesting in the belly."

Leunig

Love and Fear

There are only two feelings. Love and fear.
There are only two languages. Love and fear.
There are only two activities. Love and fear.
There are only two motives, two procedures,
two frameworks, two results. Love and fear.
Love and fear.

When the heart
Is cut or cracked or broken
Do not clutch it
Let the wound lie open;

Let the wind
From the good old sea blow in,
To bathe the wound with salt
And let it sting.

Let a stray dog lick it,
Let a bird lean in the hole and sing,
A simple song like a tiny bell
And let it ring.

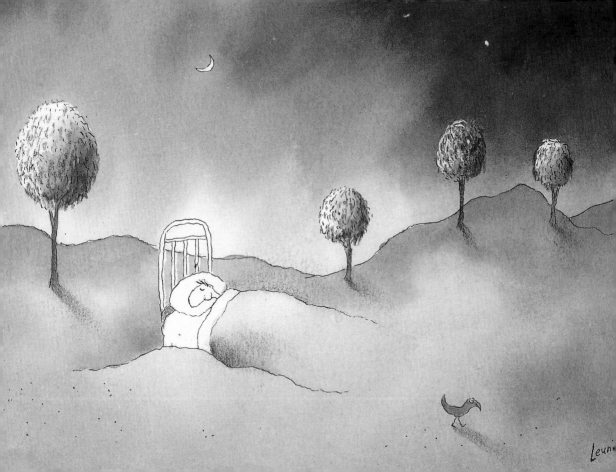